Nature of Faith

Nature of Faith

Jerry Savelle

Nature of Faith

Unless otherwise noted, all Scripture
quotations are taken from
The King James Version of the Holy Bible.

Jerry Savelle Ministries
P.O. Box 748
Crowley, TX 76036
817-297-3155

TABLE OF CONTENTS

I.   The Victorious Life of Faith   13

II.   The Levels of Faith   31

III.   Faith Sees, Speaks and Acts   41

IV.   Faith Stands, Rejoices and Rests   57

Conclusion   87

Author Bio   89

Prayer   93

Once when I was in a very adverse situation, I thought, The only way I'm going to get out of this is by having a new revelation from God. This is the revelation God gave me: "Go back to the basics."

In a letter to the Church, the Apostle Peter wrote:

"Wherefore I will not be negligent to put you always in remembrance of these things, though ye know them, and be established in the present truth. Yea, I think it meet, as long as I am in this tabernacle, to stir you up by putting you in remembrance."

2 PETER 1:12-13

Many people who are looking for new revelations should instead be building a good foundation by refreshing themselves with the basics.

Building a foundation on the basics of God's Word is like constructing a house. You don't build a foundation for a house, then destroy it; you keep building on it. When you lay hold of a basic truth of God's Word, you don't throw it away and get a new one. You keep it and add to it.

The same principles that worked for Jesus, the apostles, and other great men of faith will work for you. Get established in the basics. This is the purpose of this book: to establish you in the fundamental principles of faith. Read it over and over again until your faith cannot be shaken.

Jerry Savelle

I.

THE VICTORIOUS LIFE OF FAITH

Faith is very important.

It is our method of pleasing God. *But without faith it is impossible to please him* (Hebrews 11:6).

It is our method of victory over everything the devil throws in our paths. *"...and this is the victory that overcometh the world, even our faith"* (1 John 5:4).

God has instructed us to live by faith. *"The just shall live by faith"* (Romans 1:17). The faith life is adventurous and victorious.

The Measure of Faith

"I beseech you therefore, brethren, by the mercies of God, that ye present your bodies a living sacrifice, holy, acceptable unto God, which is your reasonable service.

And be not conformed to this world: but be ye transformed by the renewing of your mind, that ye may prove what is that good, and acceptable, and perfect, will of God.

For I say, through the grace given unto me, to every man that is among you, not to think of himself more highly than he ought to think; but to think soberly, according as God hath dealt to every man the measure of faith."

ROMANS 12:1-3

"Pray for us... that we may be delivered from unreasonable and wicked men: for all men have not faith."

2 THESSALONIANS 3:1-2

Some people are confused by these two scriptures. They say, "One verse states that every man has been given faith; the other states some men don't have faith. What did Paul mean?"

The answer is simple when you rightly divide God's Word. In Romans chapter 12 when Paul says, *"God hath dealt to every man the measure of faith,"* he is talking about the Church. He says, *"I beseech you therefore, brethren..."* and *"For I say... to every man that is among you..."* (the brethren).

In 2 Thessalonians 3 when Paul says, *"...all men have not faith,"* he is talking about the wicked men of the world, not the Church. People in the Church have been given faith; people in the world have not. To be dealt the measure of faith, you have to be born again. Ephesians 2:8-9 says, *"For by grace are ye saved through faith; and that not of yourselves: it is the gift of God: Not of works, lest any man should boast."*

15

If you have made Jesus Christ the Lord of your life, *"every man that is among you"* includes you. God has dealt you the measure of faith.

Someone may say, "Yes, but my faith will never be as great as the faith of men like Oral Roberts or T.L. Osborn. God dealt them a large measure and me a little dab."

If God deals some people more faith than others, what criteria does He use in deciding who gets how much? How do we impress God enough to get Him to give us some extra faith?

Faith is *"...not of works, lest any man should boast."* The Bible says God is just and *"no respecter of persons"* (Acts 10:34). He deals to every believer the same measure of faith.

Let's examine the meaning of metron, the Greek word for measure. Metron literally means "a determined extent; a portion taken off." The word portion implies a part or a measure of something.

Let me give you an example of "a determined extent." If I invited some people to my house for pie, I wouldn't give one person the whole pie. I would calculate how much to give each person and everyone would get exactly the same amount – a predetermined measure.

God predetermined the measure of faith He would impart to every Believer before anyone was ever born again. He gave each Believer a determined extent, a portion taken off of His own faith.

Jesus said, *"Have faith in God"* (Mark 11:22). Other translations say, "Have the faith of God" or "Have the God kind of faith." I'm convinced that the measure of faith God deals to every Believer is the God kind.

That measure of faith is the same kind that created the universe. It led three million Israelites out of bondage in Egypt and made a path of dry land across the Red Sea. It raised Jesus from the dead and has worked in the lives of the great men of faith throughout the ages.

Because these men used the measure God dealt them and followed the instructions in His Word, their faith grew. That's what makes them different from many other Christians. The measure of faith will be of no use to the person who lets it lie dormant.

Faith Grows

God does not want you to live your entire Christian experience on the measure of faith He originally dealt you. In fact, He expects you to use His Word to increase it. Romans 10:17 says, *"So then faith cometh by hearing, and hearing by the word of God."* The literal Greek says, "So faith is by report, but the report by the Word of God."

Jesus is the author of faith (Hebrews 12:2). When He talks, you hear what He says, and faith comes. Paul said, *"Not boasting of things without our measure, that is, of other men's labours; but having hope, when your faith is increased, that we shall be enlarged by you according to our rule abundantly"* (2 Corinthians 10:15).

The phrase "faith cometh" and "when your faith is increased" shows that the measure of faith God deals to believers can grow. If you compare your faith level today to what it was a year ago, you will probably find that it has grown.

One time the disciples said to Jesus, *"Increase our faith"* (Luke 17:5). He could have answered, *"It's impossible to increase faith; you've got all you'll ever get."* Instead, He taught them how to do it.

Meditate the Word

God says to meditate the Word by day and by night and to incline your ear to His sayings (Joshua 1:8; Proverbs 4:20). The number one method God has chosen for us to use in increasing our faith is to exercise this spiritual law. *"Faith cometh by hearing, and hearing by the word of God"* (Romans 10:17).

Beginning with the measure of faith residing within us, we apply this spiritual law by meditating the Word. God imparts the faith in that Word into our hearts increasing our original measure.

John 1:1 says, *"In the beginning was the Word, and the Word was with God, and the Word was God."* We can't reach out and touch God, but we can read His Word which is the same as touching God. The Word is God.

God has faith because He is the Source of faith. When we go to the Word, God gives us faith to move the mountain of need. At times, the mountain gets bigger as the need is greater. By meditating the Word, we get sufficient faith to take care of that need.

Let me warn you: Unless you have great faith operating in your heart, you will not get great faith results. Kenneth Copeland once said to me, *"Start believing God now for your next pair of socks. Don't wait until you're faced with a life or death situation to develop your faith. The same principles that get you the socks will get you healed of sickness and disease."*

If someone piled a small weight of things on your back, you would still be able to walk off easily. But as more things were piled on your back, you would have a harder time walking away. Eventually you wouldn't be able to move.

Many people are spiritually weak because they don't meditate the Word. The weight of needs piled on them cannot be dealt with by using the little faith they have. They should start developing their faith before needs begin weighing them down.

Don't Overload Your Faith

Some people misunderstand faith. When they see great accomplishments made by men of faith, they think, I'm going to do something like that. There is nothing wrong with this kind of inspiration. But when they try to do what somebody else did without being on the same faith level, they will probably fail.

One time, as God was dealing with me about faith, He said, "Son, when you started taking flying lessons, you didn't begin in a 747. You started by flying a little airplane that wasn't much faster than a lawn mower with wings.

Why? Because you weren't ready for a 747." It wouldn't have worked for me to say, "I can do all things through Christ, so I'll start out flying the 747."

Before God told me to launch out into my own ministry, I was working with Kenneth Copeland when he gave away his $38,000 airplane because he needed funds to pay for his TV ministry. About eleven days later, someone gave him the money to purchase a bigger airplane and pay cash for the TV production.

Immediately I thought, I'm going to do that! There was only one problem with my thinking that way: God's Word was not the motivating factor for me. I didn't have enough Word in me to do what he did. Fortunately, I had enough sense to wait until my faith grew.

Just a few years later I had developed my faith to the level of selling an airplane and giving all the money from the sale to different ministries. Because I was prompted by the Word and the Holy Spirit, not by someone's testimony, God blessed me with another airplane!

As a Believer, you start out as a spiritual baby with limitations. When you spend time in the Word, faith comes. As your faith increases, your limitations decrease. You notice that the things which seemed impossible six months before have become possible. Your faith has grown.

Determine Your Level of Faith

Once I asked God, "How can you detect how much your faith can handle? How do you know when to let your faith grow a little more before you set out to do something?"

To answer, God showed me a key in His Word. He reminded me of the two blind men who asked Jesus to give them their sight. Jesus asked them this question, *"Believe ye that I am able to do this?"* (Matthew 9:28). Notice in this verse that Jesus put the responsibility on them. Without hesitation they answered, "Yea, Lord."

The Spirit of God said to me, "Before you set out to do something with your faith, ask yourself this question: Do I believe God is able to do this? If you can't immediately answer, 'Yea, Lord,' you're not ready. Go to the Word and continue feeding your spirit, then ask yourself again: Do I believe God is able to do this? If you hesitate, go back to the Word and fill your spirit. When you can immediately answer, 'Yea, Lord,' you're ready. If you do this, you'll never fail."

Being around men of faith who are accomplishing great things is an inspiration to me. I think, I love the Word like they do. If the Word can get great things done in their lives, it can in mine too.

I didn't give away my airplane just because another minister gave his away. I gave away mine when the Word was so alive inside me that I was able to say without hesitation, "Yea, Lord. I believe that You can supply another one."

Faith Can Decrease

As we have already discussed, faith comes by hearing the Word. The opposite is also true. Faith goes by not hearing the Word. Jesus put it this way:

"For whosoever hath, to him shall be given, and he shall have more abundance: but whosoever hath not, from him shall be taken away even that he hath."

MATTHEW 13:12

If you choose to hear God's Word, your faith level will increase. If you choose not to hear God's Word, your faith level will drop. Even your original measure of faith will begin to diminish.

One spiritual law we have established thus far in this study is: Jesus speaks, you hear, faith comes. Now let me establish another law: The devil speaks, you hear, fear comes.

If you choose not to hear God's Word, you begin hearing what the devil is saying. By listening to the devil, fear is created in your heart because fear is the opposite of faith. Great amounts of faith and fear cannot reside in you at the same time. You have either great faith and little fear or great fear and little faith.

Job proved that great fear will bring results. He said, *"The thing which I greatly feared is come upon me"* (Job 3:25). Job was a prosperous and successful man until he started exercising fear. Then terrible things began happening to him.

If great fear brings tragedy, then great faith brings success. If fear brings heartache, faith cures heartache. If great fear destroys material possessions, great faith restores them. Fear brings sickness, faith brings health.

Taking care of your faith is like taking care of your bank account. Your heart is like a treasury. You have to deposit money into your account so that you can make withdrawals. You make deposits into your heart by hearing the Word.

If you write checks for more money than you have in your bank accounts, you will face a deficit. That means you have more money going out than is coming in.

When you use your faith, you are making withdrawals or writing checks. If you are placing more demands on your faith than you have Word in you to support them, you will face a deficit.

You make daily withdrawals on your faith. Because of this, you need to make continual deposits as well. You do that by meditating the Word day and night. Then you can make withdrawals on your faith when you need to.

You must feed your faith every day just as you feed your body. Your spirit man craves the Word as your body craves food. Don't suppress that craving.

Live on Faith in God's Word

Many times, after accomplishing something with their faith, people allow the devil to pump them full of pride. They get so busy thinking about what great faith they have that they quit meditating the Word. Then the devil brings a flood to wipe them out. They try to overcome the flood with the faith that got them over before. That won't work. God never told us to live by faith in our faith. He told us to live by faith in His Word.

Don't Live on Someone Else's Faith

In Acts 19:13-16 we read about the seven sons of Sceva who tried to cast a demon out of a man on Paul's faith. They said, *"We adjure you by Jesus whom Paul preacheth"* (v. 13). Knowing how to cast out demons was a revelation to Paul but not to the sons of Sceva. Notice what happened:

"And the evil spirit answered and said, Jesus I know, and Paul I know; but who are ye?

And the man in whom the evil spirit was leaped on them, and overcame them, and prevailed against them, so that they fled out of that house naked and wounded."

ACTS 19:15-16

The sons of Sceva lost their britches! That's what often happens to people who try to live on someone else's faith.

The Lord once showed me that a person who hasn't spent sufficient time in the Word is like a flat tire. When a problem arises, he tries to conquer it with deflated faith. He said, "You can't get anywhere on a flat tire. But air 'cometh' by pumping. When you're down, Satan tries his best to overcome you with negative circumstances. By meditating My Word, you pump faith into your spirit."

Air comes by pumping, and faith comes by hearing. If your mind is telling you that nothing is working, then your faith is flat. Begin meditating God's Word and keep on until your faith cometh. You wouldn't pump a tire half full and stop. Keep pumping up your faith until you can say, "Yea Lord, I believe You can do it."

Give the Word First Place

Romans 1:17 says, *"The just shall live by faith."* If you meditate the Word by day and by night, you will wake up in the morning praising God instead of thinking about problems. Every problem will be a challenge for the Word – another opportunity to prove that Jesus is Lord, that the Word works, and that your faith overcomes the world.

You can determine your own level of faith. How? Give the Word of God first place and make it final authority in your life.

II.

THE LEVELS OF FAITH

Jesus talked about different levels of faith and the two predominant ways of measuring them. He used a spiritual device to measure faith. He did it by judging words and actions. Let's look at an example of this in the Bible.

No Faith

In the following passage, notice what the disciples say and do when adversity comes.

"And the same day, when the even was come, he saith unto them, Let us pass over unto the other side.

And when they had sent away the multitude, they took him even as he was in the ship. And there were also with him other little ships.

And there arose a great storm of wind, and the waves beat into the ship, so that it was now full.

And he was in the hinder part of the ship, asleep on a pillow: and they awake him, and say unto him, Master, carest thou not that we perish?

And he arose, and rebuked the wind, and said unto the sea, Peace, be still. And the wind ceased, and there was a great calm.

And he said unto them, Why are ye so fearful? How is it that ye have no faith?"

MARK 4:35-40

To the disciples, Jesus said something like this:

"I'm going to measure your faith. Peter, I'll start with you. Before we entered the ship I said to you, 'Let us pass over to the other side.' I did not intend to drown. While I was asleep, a storm arose. I had given you authority to get Me to the other side, but you reacted negatively to the storm."

"I'm going to use a spiritual device, which judges words and actions, to measure your faith. The scale registers your level of faith. Your words were, 'Don't you care that we perish?' Your actions showed that you were frightened. The scale registers 'no faith.'"

"But Jesus, I'm afraid because the sea is rough and the ship is shaking!"

"The wind has ceased, Peter. You're so frightened that you didn't notice. You have no faith."

Jesus does not waste words. If he says, "How is it that ye have no faith?" then you have none.

Little Faith

Let's look at another time Jesus measured Peter's faith.

"And straightway Jesus constrained his disciples to get into a ship, and to go before him unto the other side, while he sent the multitudes away.

And when he had sent the multitudes away, he went up into a mountain apart to pray: and when the evening was come, he was there alone.

But the ship was now in the midst of the sea, tossed with waves: for the wind was contrary.

And in the fourth watch of the night Jesus went unto them, walking on the sea.

And when the disciples saw him walking on the sea, they were troubled, saying, It is a spirit; and they cried out for fear.

But straightway Jesus spake unto them, saying, Be of good cheer; it is I; be not afraid.

And Peter answered him and said, Lord, if it be thou, bid me come unto thee on the water.

And he said, Come. And when Peter was come down out of the ship, he walked on the water, to go to Jesus."

MATTHEW 14:22-29

<u>Christ speaks, you hear, faith comes.</u> Notice that when Jesus said, "Come," Peter heard Him and immediately received that word into his heart. It conceived an image of him walking on the water to Jesus, so he got out of the boat and did just that!

Some people think that the moment he got out on the water, he began to sink. That's not true. He was actually walking on the water heading for Jesus.

This time Peter was operating in great faith. If you don't believe it, fill up your bathtub and try doing what Peter did. Notice what happened to that great faith:

"But when he saw the wind boisterous, he was afraid; and beginning to sink, he cried, saying, Lord, save me.

And immediately Jesus stretched forth his hand, and caught him, and said unto him, O thou of little faith, wherefore didst thou doubt?"

MATTHEW 14:30-31

As long as Peter had his eyes on the Word, his faith was great. But when he saw that the wind was boisterous, he started to sink. When you are looking at the circumstances, you can't see the Word. You don't have the ability to consider both at the same time. You may run from one to the other, but one of them will overrule.

As Jesus reached down to pull Peter out, He said, "Peter, I'm going to measure your faith. When I said, 'Come,' you got out of the boat and responded in faith by walking on the water. The scale registered 'Great Faith.' Very good, Peter! The other day you had 'No Faith.'"

"But then you started considering the circumstances, the boisterous wind. You thought, I can't walk on the water when there is a strong wind! You were deceived, Peter. When you took your eyes off the Word, you began to sink.

Then you cried out, 'Save me!' The scale now registers, 'Little Faith.'"

Peter had shown improvement. In the first situation he had "No Faith" and in the second "Little Faith." It's better to have little faith than none.

Great Faith

In Matthew 8:5-8, Jesus measured a centurion's faith:

"And when Jesus was entered into Capernaum, there came unto him a centurion, beseeching him,

And saying, Lord, my servant lieth at home sick of the palsy, grievously tormented.

And Jesus saith unto him, I will come and heal him.

The centurion answered and said, Lord, I am not worthy that thou shouldest come under my roof: but speak the word only, and my servant shall be healed."

"When Jesus heard it," (what the centurion said) "he marveled, and said to them that followed, Verily I say unto you, I have

not found so great faith, no not in Israel" (v. 10). Jesus was saying, *"What the centurion said and did is causing the scale's indicator to rise fast. It registers 'Great Faith.' This is the greatest faith I've ever seen!"*

After Jesus rose from the dead, He measured Thomas' faith. When the other disciples told Thomas that they had seen Jesus, Thomas said,

"Except I shall see in his hands the print of the nails, and put my finger into the print of the nails, and thrust my hand into his side, I will not believe."

JOHN 20:25

Later, Jesus appeared to them and said to Thomas, *"Reach hither thy finger, and behold my hands; and reach hither thy hand, and thrust it into my side: and be not faithless, but believing"* (John 20:27). In other words, Jesus was saying if you have to feel or see something first, your level of faith is "No Faith."

The indicator on the scale will rise fast if you react to sickness by saying, "The Word is my final authority. It says that I am healed by the stripes of Jesus. That's all the evidence I need. I'm healed and that settles it!" Jesus will marvel at your faith.

Immeasurable Faith

Let's look at another level of faith that Jesus measured. The Apostle Paul wrote to the Thessalonian church:

"Grace unto you, and peace, from God our Father and the Lord Jesus Christ.

We are bound to thank God always for you, brethren, as it is meet, because that your faith groweth exceedingly..."

2 THESSALONIANS 1:2-3

The Greek word for exceedingly is perissos which means "superabundantly above, beyond measure." You can get to such a high level that your faith becomes immeasurable.

The Thessalonians' faith was so great that Paul said:

"For from you sounded out the word of the Lord not only in Macedonia and Achaia, but also in every place your faith to God-ward is spread abroad; so that we need not to speak any thing."

1 THESSALONIANS 1:8

Paul was saying, "Everywhere I go, people have heard about your faith. I don't even get to tell the story anymore. <u>You have become the sounding board for faith</u>."

Today, we Christians should be the sounding board for faith. The only way you can develop your faith to an immeasurable point is by applying the law: *<u>"Faith cometh by hearing, and hearing by the word of God"</u>* (Romans 10:17).

Whether you have "No Faith" or "Little Faith," if you want more, simply meditate the Word. When faith comes, your measure grows and the limitations decrease. Finally, you reach this point: *"All things are possible to him that believeth"* (Mark 9:23).

III.

FAITH SEES, SPEAKS & ACTS

Believers need to learn how to operate in the full cycle of faith. Let's examine the basic characteristics of faith.

Faith Sees the Image

First, faith sees the end result before it can be seen in the natural realm. Every good thing that comes to pass in your life starts in your heart – your spirit. Jesus said, *"A good man out of the good treasure of the heart bringeth forth good things..."* (Matthew 12:35).

"The spirit of man is the candle of the Lord..."

PROVERBS 20:27

Your spirit is creative and productive like God. Functioning much like a manufacturing plant, your spirit forms an image programming you with what you can rightfully have and do.

God designed His Word to create an image in your heart. Words paint pictures, images. When you hear the word dog, you picture a dog.

When you meditate the Word and allow the Holy Spirit to join with you in your studying, He will use the Word of God like oil to paint a picture, an image of what God is saying on the canvas of your heart. If you need money, start creating an image of yourself with money by meditating God's Word. Confess the scriptures that promise to meet your financial needs.

Meditate on verses like this one: *"But my God shall supply all your need according to his riches in glory by Christ Jesus"* (Philippians 4:19). God will paint a picture on the canvas of your heart of your needs being met. That image will be more real than what your physical eyes see.

Faith Sees the Unseen

God saw an image of the universe inside Himself before He ever spoke. He saw man before He created him. Genesis 1:27 says, *"God created man in his own image."* He conceived an image of man, then created him by following that pattern or blueprint. Paul wrote:

"While we look not at the things which are seen, but at the things which are not seen: for the things which are seen are temporal; but the things which are not seen are eternal."

2 CORINTHIANS 4:18

"For we walk by faith, not by sight."

2 CORINTHIANS 5:7

Paul is implying that the Believer is not to be governed by what he sees in the physical realm.

The Highest Form of Reality

Hebrews 11:1 says, *"Now faith is the substance of things hoped for, the evidence of things not seen."* Once you have conceived

43

the image, faith is the evidence that what you need exists. Something you have evidence for exists whether it is visible or not. You can't see your brain, but it exists.

The unseen realm is not a fantasy world in which you pretend certain things exist; it deals with facts. The highest form of reality that exists is this: God's Word is true.

When you look beyond the problem, you are seeing with the eye of faith. The physical eye sees only temporal things. The eye of faith looks beyond that which is seen – the problem, the circumstances – and sees the unseen.

Hebrews 12:2 says, *"...for the joy that was set before him"* (Jesus) *"endured the cross..."* To the natural eye, Calvary looked like defeat. But Jesus had joy because He saw the end result beyond the torture of the cross. He knew He would destroy the devil's power and give the earth a new class of men.

Getting hold of this idea will revolutionize your life. Everything that your physical eye can see is subject to change. Jesus proved it in His own ministry.

Jesus Looked Beyond the Problem

According to what the physical eyes can see, over five thousand men, women and children cannot be fed with five loaves and two fishes. Jesus proved this was subject to change. Matthew 14:17-21 describes how He multiplied the loaves and fishes to feed the multitude of people.

First, He took His eyes off the circumstances and looked up to heaven. Then, He blessed the food, broke it and handed it to His disciples. They had the pleasure of passing out what originally couldn't be seen.

Luke 13:10-13 tells of the woman bowed over with a spirit of infirmity. When she entered a synagogue where Jesus was preaching, He saw beyond the problem and said, *"Woman, thou art loosed from thine infirmity"* (v. 12). He had an image of her standing strong and tall. The woman took hold of that image and walked out healed.

You need to see beyond what other people see. When I was preparing to build new facilities for our ministry, I saw buildings on the property and thousands of people being blessed and set free. Other people saw nothing but an empty lot. The Spirit of God had not conceived in their hearts the image He had conceived in mine.

Elisha Saw the Unseen

When Elisha, the prophet of God, was surrounded by enemy forces, he said to his servant, *"Fear not: for they that be with us are more than they that be with them"* (2 Kings 6:16). The prophet was seeing beyond the physical evidence.

Elisha's servant must have been confused. With his natural eyes he saw only the two of them and that they were surrounded. Finally, Elisha said, *"LORD, I pray thee, open his eyes, that he may see"* (v. 17). The servant was then able to see that the mountain was full of angels. There were *"horses and chariots of fire round about Elisha"* (v. 17).

See From God's Viewpoint

Many Christians are too involved in seeing with their physical eyes. They let themselves be controlled by the circumstances – the zero recorded in their checkbooks, their worn-out cars, the symptoms in their bodies, their ornery husbands or wives. They can't see beyond the problem in front of them.

When they begin meditating the Word, they begin seeing what God sees and looking at life from His viewpoint. Though their husbands or wives act terrible and never seem close to getting saved, they can smile and say, "Things which are seen are subject to change."

They get in their old, worn-out car, pat the seats, and say, "Praise God, before long, I'll be driving a better car. I can see it through the eye of faith." Soon the image becomes more real than what they see with their physical eyes.

Let God's Word, instead of the evening news, form the image. The only reason I pick up a newspaper or watch the news is to see what I'm redeemed from.

I would like to hear a newscaster say, "Our nation is faced with a tremendous crisis. But we're not moved by what we see. Thanks be unto God Who gives us the victory through Christ Jesus!"

Some people read the Bible from a religious standpoint reading only a portion of Scripture and missing the truth. For instance, Psalm 34:19 says, *"Many are the afflictions of the righteous: but the LORD delivereth him out of them all."* The word "but" is a conjunction; it connects two thoughts. Some people stop reading after the first part, *"Many are the afflictions of the righteous..."* This paints an entirely different picture from the truth. These people see themselves afflicted instead of seeing themselves delivered out of all the afflictions.

In John 16:33 Jesus said, *"...In the world ye shall have tribulation: but be of good cheer; I have overcome the world."* When people stop reading after the first part, they see themselves being of great sorrow instead of good cheer. When you are reading the Bible, put off religious thinking. Otherwise, you might form an image not based on truth.

Overcome the Defeat Image

Some people can't see themselves healed. John 5:2-9 tells of the lame man who sat by the pool of Bethesda for thirty-eight years. At certain times an angel troubled the water of the pool. Whoever stepped immediately into the pool was healed of his disease.

Because the man was crippled, someone always stepped into the pool before him. He didn't expect to recover, but he sat by the pool because it was his last hope. He had a defeat image, a crippled image; he couldn't see himself healed.

Jesus always ministered to people in this order: spirit, soul and body. He realized that the man was sick not only physically, but inside, too. To get the man healed, He first had to change the image in the man's heart. Proverbs 12:25 says, *"Heaviness in the heart of man maketh it stoop: but a good word maketh it glad."*

Jesus reached the spirit man first and changed the man's inner image by giving him a good word. The greatest word the man could hear was, "Rise." Jesus spoke that good word and made the man's heart glad. Immediately his image changed on the inside. Even though he had been crippled for thirty-eight years, he could see himself getting up.

Jesus was saying to the man's spirit, "Change your image." To the man's soul, "Change your attitude. Quit seeing yourself being carried around on a bed; start seeing yourself carrying the bed." To the man's body He said, "Take up your bed and walk." The man's spirit rose, his soul changed attitudes and his body walked.

Meditate the Word and see yourself as God sees you. You are a joint-heir with Jesus (Romans 8:17). Whatever He gets, you get. You are a winner – more than a conqueror and an overcomer (Romans 8:37; 1 John 5:4). No weapon formed against you prospers (Isaiah 65:17). The angel of the Lord encamps around about you and delivers you (Psalm 34:7).

God sees you healed and blessed. He sees you controlling circumstances and reigning in life – not allowing life to reign over you! Paul said, *"I believed, and therefore have I spoken"* (2 Corinthians 4:13).

When you see the image inside you and believe it, you will speak it automatically. Creative words will come out of your spirit. Be careful to conceive the right kind of image in your heart. Jesus said, *"...out of the abundance of the heart the mouth speaketh. A good man out of the good treasure of the heart bringeth forth good things: and an evil man out of the evil treasure bringeth forth evil things"* (Matthew 12:34-35).

You will talk about the image you have conceived, either good or bad. If you have a failure image, you will talk failure. If you have a poverty image, you will talk poverty. When you talk the image, good or bad, you can have what you say. Jesus said:

"...That whosoever shall say unto this mountain, Be thou removed, and be thou cast into the sea; and shall not doubt in his heart, but shall believe that those things which he saith shall come to pass; he shall have whatsoever he saith."

MARK 11:23

If bad things are happening to you and you want to know why, listen to what you are saying. You may think, But I just can't make good confessions. Yes, you can. You just need to change the image in your heart.

A person who continually curses can't help it. He is speaking what is in his heart in abundance. In the same way, a person who gets God's Word in his heart in abundance will have no problem talking like God. His only problem will be in finding a way to stop! When you are full of God's Word, it comes out. John 7:38 says that out of your belly shall flow rivers (not just trickles!) of living water.

Faith Sees Before It Speaks

Many people try talking faith without having conceived an image in their spirits first. Because they haven't seen that reality, what they are saying doesn't come to pass. Then they say that the faith confession doesn't work: "I've confessed that I'm healed, but I'm still sick."

They are still sick probably because they didn't conceive an image of being well first. *"For as he" (a man) "thinketh in his heart, so is he"* (Proverbs 23:7).

Jesus said that men's hearts will fail them for fear of what is coming on the earth (Luke 21:26). This statement literally means that men will die of heart attacks because of fear, but it also means the spirits of men who don't operate in faith will fail to produce. Confession is vital, but only part of the full cycle of faith.

Faith Acts

Once you have spoken the image, you begin to act accordingly. Peter saw an image of himself getting out of the boat and walking on the water to Jesus. Next, he spoke the image. He said, *"Lord, if it be thou, bid me come unto thee on the water"* (Matthew 14:28).

When Jesus said, *"Come"* (v. 29), Peter began walking on the water. Peter's faith saw, spoke and acted. But he allowed the circumstances to change his image. When he got his eyes off the unseen and onto the seen, he began to sink.

When circumstances are against you, you have to be bold with your actions and use what I call the "ripping-off-the-roof" kind of faith. Let's look at an example of this in the Bible.

Luke 5:18-20 tells of four men who took their sick friend to Jesus for healing. After conceiving an image of getting their friend to Jesus, they made the journey carrying the man on a stretcher.

When they reached the building where Jesus was preaching, they found it was full of people, and they couldn't get in. Instead of saying, *"Sometimes this faith stuff works and sometimes it doesn't; we tried our best, but couldn't get in,"* they sought *"means" (plural, not singular) "to bring him in"* (v. 18). They didn't look at the circumstances. They saw, spoke, then acted.

"And when they could not find by what way they might bring him in because of the multitude, they went upon the housetop, and let him down through the tiling with his couch into the midst before Jesus" (Luke 5:19).

Those men were bold with their faith. They ripped off the roof to get their friend to Jesus! *"And when he saw their*

faith, he said unto him, Man, thy sins are forgiven thee" (v. 20).
When Jesus saw their faith and their actions, He healed
the man.

Let faith operate this way in your life. Once you see an
image, don't let anything stop you. Start speaking it, then
take action.

Use "ripping-off-the-roof" kind of faith to "seek means." If
every door you come to is shut, don't quit. Keep knocking
on doors until one finally opens. Jesus will see your faith
and meet your need.

IV.

FAITH STANDS, REJOICES & RESTS

One time somebody said to me, "I have symptoms of sickness. I've meditated the Word and have let it create an image on the canvas of my heart. Once I began to see myself healed, I talked the image. Over and over I confessed, 'By His stripes I am healed.' Next, I started acting healed. I've got only one problem: I'm still sick! What do I do now?"

I told him that he needed to learn how to put the full cycle of faith into operation. Faith sees, speaks and acts, but it also stands, rejoices and rests. Once you get a revelation of this, you will never be defeated again.

Faith Stands

"Finally, my brethren, be strong in the Lord, and in the power of his might. Put on the whole armour of God, that ye may be able to stand against the wiles of the devil.

For we wrestle not against flesh and blood, but against principalities, against powers, against the rulers of the darkness of this world, against spiritual wickedness in high places.

Wherefore take unto you the whole armour of God, that ye may be able to withstand in the evil day, and having done all, to stand.

Stand therefore, having your loins girt about with truth, and having on the breastplate of righteousness;

And your feet shod with the preparation of the gospel of peace;

Above all, taking the shield of faith, wherewith ye shall be able to quench all the fiery darts of the wicked.

And take the helmet of salvation, and the sword of the Spirit, which is the word of God."

EPHESIANS 6:10-17

When you have seen the image, spoken it, and acted accordingly, but the circumstances haven't changed, put on the whole armor of God and stand. When you are in trouble, God hears you. So you must keep standing on His Word regardless of the circumstances.

"The LORD hear thee in the day of trouble; the name of the God of Jacob defend thee;

Send thee help from the sanctuary, and strengthen thee out of Zion;

Remember all thy offerings, and accept thy burnt sacrifice; Selah.

Grant thee according to thine own heart, and fulfil all thy counsel.

We will rejoice in thy salvation, and in the name of our God we will set up our banners: the LORD fulfil all thy petitions.

Now know I that the LORD saveth his anointed; he will hear him from his holy heaven with the saving strength of his right hand.

Some trust in chariots, and some in horses: but we will remember the name of the LORD our God.

They are brought down and fallen: but we are risen, and stand upright.

Save, LORD: let the king hear us when we call."

Psalm 20

Notice again: "They are brought down and fallen: but we are risen, and stand upright." When everything around you indicates that you can't possibly win, stand.

In the life of faith, there is no room for compromise. If you say, "I'll try this, but if it doesn't work, I can always use Plan B," you will always end up using Plan B.

You must be determined to win. When you say, "I'll try," you are telling the devil you have a fifty-fifty chance. Don't try to live by faith. Do it. Let go of all carnal plans.

"Moreover, brethren, I declare unto you the gospel which I preached unto you, which also ye have received, and wherein ye stand."

1 CORINTHIANS 15:1

Stand on the Gospel you have received.

"Watch ye, stand fast in the faith, quit you like men, be strong."

1 CORINTHIANS 16:13

You cannot be like the men of the world who lean on natural, carnal things. When pressure comes and the adversary tells them, "There's no way out," these men have no strength.

Strong men are men like the Apostle Paul who said, *"And being fully persuaded that, what he had promised, he was able also to perform"* (Romans 4:21). I am confident to walk by faith and not by sight (2 Corinthians 5:7). I know in whom I have believed (2 Timothy 1:12). Paul was a confident, secure man of faith and strength.

Some people think that the faith life is an insecure way to live. The insecure people are the ones who don't know the Word. God said, *"My covenant will I not break, nor alter the thing that is gone out of my lips"* (Psalm 89:34). God is not a liar!

If you are full of the Word, you always know what God will do in every area of your life. If you do what God tells you, then be assured that He will do exactly what He says in His Word. How He goes about it is His business.

When you try to figure out what avenue He will use to fulfill His Word, you are playing God. For example, you might say, "God, in Luke 6:38, You say that when I give, men shall give unto my bosom. I've given, so men will give unto my bosom." Instead of letting God take over from there, you start trying to put faces on those men.

When you spot someone dressed nicely and driving a fine car, you think, God will probably use that man to give me the money I need to build my church.

God has to fold His hands until you quit playing His part. When you finally say, "I cast all of my care over on You, Lord," He says, "That's what I've been waiting for." He takes over and brings the manifestation about in surprising ways.

Be strong:

"Moreover I call God for a record upon my soul, that to spare you I came not as yet unto Corinth. Not for that we have dominion over your faith, but are helpers of your joy: for by faith ye stand."

2 CORINTHIANS 1:23-24

Stand in the faith:

"Therefore, my brethren dearly beloved and longed for, my joy and crown, so stand fast in the Lord, my dearly beloved."

PHILIPPIANS 4:1

Stand fast:

"Stand fast therefore in the liberty wherewith Christ hath made us free..."

GALATIANS 5:1

How long do you have to stand? Until you win. When do you win? When you don't have to stand anymore - when you get what you are believing for. If you are tired of standing, stand some more.

Many people don't know how to stand because they have been programmed by the world to be quitters. The world says, "When the going gets tough, quit." The Bible implies, "When the going gets tough, stand."

Don't Quit

"Cast not away therefore your confidence, which hath great recompence of reward."

HEBREWS 10:35

Confidence means faith. Cast not away your faith. Your greatest opportunity to compromise comes when you have done all you know to do and are standing on God's Word. By creating bad circumstances, the devil tries to get you to cast away your faith and quit.

If you become so weary, lazy or angry that you take your faith off the job, you will let the problem overtake you. As long as you are offering resistance, you still have a chance to win.

The J.B. Phillips version of the Bible translates Ephesians 6:13 as *"...when you have fought to a standstill... still stand your ground."*

A standstill happens when two opposing forces refuse to move. When you reach a standstill with Satan, one of you will have to compromise and give in. Satan is a compromiser, a loser by nature.

He knows he can't win and that he is headed for the lake of fire. He is a bully and a bluff, but he doesn't want you to know that. When you stand your ground with a bully, he runs.

Keep standing. Keep quenching those fiery darts with your shield of faith. If Satan can't get through to you with his attacks, he will try to create pressure by assigning a messenger to you.

He doesn't send a sinner. He sends a Bible-toting, tongue-talking, church-going saint who doesn't know anything about standing. The messenger starts telling you about the bad things that happened to him when he tried to do what you are doing. He tries to draw negative confessions out of you.

"Has your prayer been answered yet?" He asks.

"I believe that I receive," you answer.

Sometimes it's hard to convince people that what you have laid hold of with your faith exists. But they can't argue with the result when they see it in the natural realm.

There are three keys to success:

1. Find out what the will of God is.

2. Confer not with flesh and blood.

3. Get the job done at any cost.

Get hold of number two. When Satan sends the negative person, confer no more with flesh and blood. Put on your earplugs and your helmet of salvation. Look the person straight in the eye, smile and say to yourself, I'm not moved by what I hear. After a while, he will either leave or start agreeing with you. You don't want to lose ground. You want to be reinforced.

Deuteronomy 32:30 says that one can put one thousand to flight and two can put ten thousand to flight. Get reinforcements. Find people to agree with you as you stand and gang up on the devil.

If you can't find anybody to stand with you, realize that you and God are the majority. With God, stand your ground.

When you have fought to a standstill, remember that the devil is a flub. He will try to convince you that he isn't giving up. If you fall for it and run off, you will lose ground. All you have to do is hit him with your sword (the spoken Word). He will flee in stark terror.

Have Patience

"Cast not away therefore your confidence, which hath great recompence of reward.

For ye have need of patience, that, after ye have done the will of God, ye might receive the promise.

For yet a little while, and he that shall come will come, and will not tarry.

Now the just shall live by faith: but if any man draw back, my soul shall have no pleasure in him."

HEBREWS 10:35-38

After you have stood, you have need of patience. Some people don't like the word patience because they have a warped definition of it. They think patience means putting up with a problem until it gets better. Jesus never put up with any problem. He dominated problems. He never tolerated the devil. He controlled him.

Patience means to be consistent, constant and unchanging regardless of the circumstances. The confession of the patient man is always the same. Whether he has money or needs it, he says, "My God meets my need according to His riches in glory."

A patient man is like God *"with whom is no variableness, neither shadow of turning"* (James 1:17). God says, *"I change not."* The members of the Body of Christ should also say, "I change not."

69

When the devil throws another dart at you and asks, "What are you going to do now?" You answer, *"I have declared what I believe. My God meets my needs. I am not afraid of evil tidings. My heart is fixed, established, trusting in the Lord. I will not be moved until I see my desire upon my enemy. I change not!"* (See Philippians 4:19; Psalms 112:7-8)

"Knowing this, that the trying of your faith worketh patience.

But let patience have her perfect work, that ye may be perfect and entire, wanting nothing."

JAMES 1:3-4

The trying of faith should trigger patience. But this doesn't happen for people who don't know how to respond when pressure comes. They fold up and quit by casting away their faith. They watch TV or sleep to find refuge from pressure. The problem is that when they turn off the TV or wake up, the pressure is still there.

Once you have released your faith, Satan comes immediately to try it. But God counteracts that attempt with a trigger mechanism He has put inside you. When the devil tries your faith, God causes the trigger mechanism to go off in your spirit to release patience or consistency to support your faith.

"Let patience have her perfect work" means let patience do what it is designed to do: cause you to be stable, unwavering, consistent, constant and unchanging. When you let patience support your faith and cause you to maintain stability, you will be "perfect and entire, wanting nothing." When you want nothing, you possess what you were believing for.

Don't Waver

"But let him ask in faith, nothing wavering. For he that wavereth is like a wave of the sea driven with the wind and tossed.

For let not that man think that he shall receive any thing of the Lord.

A double minded man is unstable in all his ways."

JAMES 1:6-8

You must become single-minded and unwavering about what you believe God's Word is saying you can have. Don't let any of these negative people Satan sends talk you out of what you know is yours.

Weymouth's New Testament in Modern Speech translates verse eight as "a man of two minds, undecided in every step he takes."

One time a woman with symptoms of sickness asked, "Brother Jerry, would you lay hands on me? I believe that according to Mark 16:18 I'll recover."

After I laid hands on her and prayed, I said, "Tell me what you believe."

"I believe I'm healed," she said. "But do you think I should go to the hospital just in case?"

"Yes, if I were you, I'd go right now because you're going to need it."

She was double-minded.

Faith stands. It is consistent, not moved by circumstances. When you become double-minded, you waver because you are unstable. There is no consistency in your life.

Many people go through life like a "wave of the sea driven with the wind and tossed." One moment a double-minded man says, "My God meets my needs." The next moment he says, "Oh, dear God, I'm going broke." One moment, he says, "I believe I'm healed." The next moment, he says, "I don't feel healed – I hurt." He walks through his entire life unstable like this. One good wind will finish him off.

When the pressure comes, don't turn on the TV or go to sleep. Go to the Word. God is our refuge (Psalms 46:1).

While the devil is creating pressure, God is telling you, "Come on, you can do it! I've equipped you to do it!" He will encourage, not discourage you. Become stable by planting both feet on the Rock of your salvation, Jesus Christ.

Faith Rejoices

Let's return to our examination of James chapter 1.

"My brethren, count it all joy when ye fall into divers temp-
tations; Knowing this, that the trying of your faith worketh
patience. But let patience have her perfect work, that ye may be
perfect and entire, wanting nothing."

JAMES 1:2-4

When you are under Satan's attack, maintain an attitude
of joy. Don't let Satan discourage you. Don't let pressure
or anything else take your joy. If Satan steals your joy, he
will get your strength. If you are weak, you won't be able
to resist. At times, when nothing seems to be working out,
you get under such severe pressure that you almost wonder
if God has forsaken you.

You are dressed in the full armor of God, holding your
shield of faith to quench every fiery dart, but your shield is
getting so heavy with darts that you can hardly hold it up.
Your helmet is about to fall off. The rivets start coming out
of your breastplate. Your belt won't stay tight. Your shoes
become slick, and your feet start sliding out from under

you. Your sword has become dull. When you started, it was sharp.

At first you said, "My God meets my needs!" Now you are asking, "My God meets my needs?" Worn out, you look at your shield full of darts and think, If the devil fires one more dart, I've had it.

Once when this happened to me, God said, "Now is the time for rejoicing."

"What is there to rejoice about?" I asked.

"Son, you've got the devil right where you want him."

I thought, I do? It didn't look like it to me; but God said I did, so I began to praise Him and rejoice. Immediately, I heard something whistling through the wind. It wasn't a dart. It was a missile zooming straight toward my shield!

"I thought You said I had the devil right where I wanted him," I shouted.

"You do," God answered. "Start rejoicing."

"Why should I? A missile is coming!"

"Son, that is a good sign. I'll let you in on a Bible secret that the devil doesn't like told. When you are under the most severe pressure, the devil has just fired his best shot. If it doesn't get you, he's finished."

When I heard that, it was easy to say, "Glory to God! Hallelujah!"

Give Thanks

"As ye have therefore received Christ Jesus the Lord, so walk ye in him:

Rooted and built up in him, and stablished in the faith, as ye have been taught, abounding therein with thanksgiving."

COLOSSIANS 2:6-7

We are to abound in thanksgiving. Praise and thanksgiving is the highest expression of faith. After you pray and believe you have received, immediately thank God and rejoice.

Someone may say, "I've seen, spoken, acted and stood, but I have no reason to rejoice. It's not working." It is working. You may not be able to see the results in the natural realm, but in the spiritual realm the Holy Spirit and your angels are at work. The Word is doing your fighting. Your faith is out there eating away at that mountain of need.

Waiting until the manifestation comes before thanking God is backwards. If someone said to me, "I'm going to buy you a suit," I would say, "Thank you." I hadn't received the suit, but my thanksgiving was an expression of my faith in the person's integrity.

If I had answered, "Just as soon as you give me the suit, I'll thank you," I doubt that I would have been given the suit. Why should you expect God to give you the manifestation when you act as rudely toward Him?

The Bible says that praise will cause the earth to yield her increase (Psalms 67:5-6). Praise keeps the enemy standing still and opens the door to the blessings of God.

Faith Rests

Hebrews 4:11 says, *"Let us labour therefore to enter into that rest..."* The labor is conceiving the image. You may have to spend a few nights confessing God's Word until you get the image inside you. You don't always have to do that, but if that's what it takes to win, be willing to do it.

Sometimes when you lie down to go to sleep, the devil starts harassing you. Over and over he says, "It won't work. You'll never get what you're believing for." When that happens, you have to get up and labor.

You shouldn't mind missing some sleep when you can change things in a few hours by conceiving an image. Then you reach a point in your faith where the labor is over and you rest. Some people continue struggling with their faith never entering into that rest. They struggle because they don't let the nature, the characteristics, the full cycle of faith be operative in their lives.

"Let us therefore fear, lest, a promise being left us of entering into his rest, any of you should seem to come short of it.

For unto us was the gospel preached, as well as unto them: but the word preached did not profit them, not being mixed with faith in them that heard it.

For we which have believed do enter into rest..."

HEBREWS 4:1-3

Once you have conceived the image by seeing the end result with the eye of faith, you have spoken and acted accordingly and you have stood and rejoiced, then just enter into that rest. You will have a consuming assurance that the struggle is over and what you are believing for is yours. Because you know it is yours, you can go on to bigger and better things.

When the devil tries to bother you, laugh at him. Say, *"Devil, I'm not talking to you about it. It's mine. I don't have a worry."* When you are fully persuaded that what God has promised, He is able to perform, you rest (Romans 4:21).

Paddling Up River

The Lord gave me an illustration of the life of faith. It's like going up river in a canoe against the current. In the natural realm, there is no way to do it because everything is against you.

The world floats down river in a negative current which ends in destruction (hell). When a person is born, he begins to live like the world following the negative current. He can't help it. He's spiritually dead.

The Gospel of the Lord Jesus Christ is the only thing that can turn his boat around and head him in the right direction. The moment he hears and accepts the Gospel, he becomes a new creation. He is saved and delivered from the destiny of hell.

In the life of faith a person hears the Good News and is converted. Faith arises inside him. He wants to turn his canoe around and head up river. To do that, he has to put forth some effort.

When he was going down river, he was carried by the current. To go up river, he must turn the canoe around and paddle against the natural current. He paddles until he gets the boat turned at a ninety-degree angle to the flow of the river – a perfect position for shipwreck.

With the water beating against his boat, he thinks, I can't do it, and throws down the paddle. He lets the canoe return to flow with the current. Even though he loves God, he goes back to living like the world.

Depressed, he paddles his canoe to a Bible seminar where he learns he can have what he says. He comes alive and again spins the canoe around to a ninety-degree angle. He says, "I can have what I say. I will turn this boat around in the name of Jesus." Finally, he turns the canoe completely around.

With the water beating against his boat, debris and trash coming at him from every direction, he starts looking at the obstacles. In fear he thinks, Something could knock a hole in my ship. I'll die! He stops paddling and lets the canoe spin back around. Even though he still loves God and is going to heaven, he starts living like the world again.

He paddles his canoe to another seminar where he learns how to keep headed up river. Again, he spins his canoe around. This time, when he spots the obstacles, he says, "I'm not moved by what I see or feel," and they pass him by.

Just when things seem to be going along easier, the family starts to fuss. Often the wife is first in the family to begin living the life of faith. She paddles the canoe while her husband sits in the back and gripes, "Everything was running smoothly before you got religion. But now the boat is rocking, the table is shaking, and I'm losing my beer! Where did you get all these tapes and books? Is that where all my money has been going?"

Finally, she can't take it anymore and hits him in the head with her oar! While they are fighting, she stops paddling and the canoe spins around again. (Strife will turn your canoe around fast!)

Full of condemnation, she paddles the canoe to another seminar where she hears about the love of God and about winning your loved ones to Jesus. Again she sets her course up river. This time, instead of being upset by her husband's griping, she says, "Love never fails. Things which are seen are subject to change."

Her two kids, who are on drugs, nearly fall out of the canoe. But she manages to hold them in to keep them from drowning and paddles the canoe at the same time.

An ark from the First Church floats past headed down river. As it passes, the captain (pastor) yells, "Lady, you can't go up river. We tried it and almost died. Look at the holes in our boat. That faith stuff doesn't work." She begins to think about what he said. If the First Church can't do it, neither can I. Then the canoe turns around.

After a while, she paddles her canoe to another seminar and learns how to hold fast her confession of faith. Again she spins the canoe around and sets her course up river in the right direction. This time, another believer paddles his boat beside hers to encourage her. While they are talking, someone leads her husband to the Lord.

"Sweetheart," her husband says, "I have my own oar; let me help you." So he moves to the front of the canoe and begins to paddle. The woman's faith walk is becoming easier. She is still struggling to keep the kids in the canoe, but her husband is helping her paddle. Finally, the kids give their lives to the Lord, and they start paddling, too.

Now the whole family is operating together in the full cycle of faith. Since they have become dangerous to the devil, he starts to send obstacles. First he puts symptoms of sickness on the husband. Though he is hurting, the man says, "I'm not moved by what I feel. God's Word says that by Jesus' stripes I'm healed." Refusing to give in to the symptoms in his body, he continues to paddle the canoe, and he receives his healing.

The whole family is living in divine health so the devil attacks their finances. They fall behind in their payments on the canoe. But then the husband learns how to give his way out of debt. With their faith out against every obstacle, the family continues to move up river through life when everyone else said it couldn't be done.

Then one day the canoe paddling becomes easy. They no longer have to struggle to go up river. They are able to rest. The Spirit of God has put a sail on their boat, and He has blown it forward with a rushing, mighty wind.

In these last days, don't be surprised if God jet-propels your canoe.

CONCLUSION

I began this book by sharing a simple revelation God gave me. He said, "Go back to the basics." That's what I have endeavored to do within these pages.

To successfully live the life of faith, we must understand faith – what it is and how it works. Don't take God's faith principles for granted.

Go back and read this book again and again until you know beyond any doubt what it means to live the victorious, faith-filled, joyful life that God intends for you.

Bio: Jerry Savelle

Dr. Jerry Savelle was an average, blue-collar man who was struggling and needed God's help. While he considered himself a "nobody," when he became a believer God told him not to worry about it because He was a master at making champions out of nobodies. God has since taken Dr. Savelle from being a constant quitter to a man who knows how to stand on the Word of God until victory is experienced. Because of the life-changing combination of God's faithfulness and Dr. Savelle's "no quit" attitude, his life is totally different than it was forty years ago.

Since 1969, Dr. Savelle has been traveling the world teaching people how to win in life. Dr. Savelle has ministered in more than three thousand churches and in twenty-six nations, and has overseas offices in the United Kingdom, Australia, and Canada.

God has used Dr. Savelle to impact people who are burned out on religion and who have backslidden in their walk with God, as well as Christians who have a need to hear the Word of God presented in terms applicable to their lives, dreams, and destinies. He is the host of the Jerry Savelle Ministries television broadcast which airs in two hundred countries worldwide.

Dr. Savelle is the author of fifty-five books, including, *If Satan Can't Steal Your Joy, He Can't Keep Your Goods and Living In The Fullness Of The Blessing*, and his recent bestseller, *Called To Battle Destined To Win*. He and his wife, Carolyn, also serve as founding Pastors of Heritage of Faith Christian Center in Crowley, Texas.

Prayer of Salvation

If you were to die today, where would you spend eternity?
If you have accepted Jesus Christ as your Lord and Savior,
you can be assured that when you die, you will go directly
into the presence of God in Heaven. If you have not accepted Jesus as your personal Lord and Savior, is there
any reason why you can't make Jesus the Lord of your life
right now? Please pray this prayer out loud, and as you do,
pray with a sincere and trusting heart, and you will be born
again.

Dear God in Heaven,
I come to you in the Name of Jesus to receive salvation
and eternal life. I believe that Jesus is Your Son. I believe
that He died on the cross for my sins, and that you raised
him from the dead. I receive Jesus now into my life. Jesus,
come into my heart. I welcome you as my Lord and Savior.
I confess with my mouth that I am saved and born again. I
am now a child of God. Amen.

Other Books by Jerry Savelle

Called To Battle, Destined To Win
Living In The Fullness Of The Blessing
Increase God's Way
Receive God's Best
Free to be Yourself
The God of the Breakthrough Will Visit Your House
If Satan Can't Steal Your Dreams, He Can't
Control Your Destiny
Free at Last from Oppression
Free at Last from Old Habits
Thoughts – The Battle between Your Ears
Expect the Extraordinary
In the Footsteps of a Prophet
The Last Frontier
Take Charge of Your Financial Destiny
From Devastation to Restoration
Turning Your Adversity into Victory
Honoring Your Heritage of Faith
Don't Let Go of Your Dreams
Faith Building Daily Devotionals
The Force of Joy
If Satan Can't Steal Your Joy, He Can't
Keep Your Goods
A Right Mental Attitude
The Nature of Faith
Sharing Jesus Effectively
How to Overcome Financial Famine
You're Somebody Special to God
The Established Heart